Swamp Cookin'
with the
River People

DANA HOLYFIELD

Ten Speed Press
Berkeley, California

Ten Speed Press
P.O. Box 7123
Berkeley, California 94707
www.tenspeed.com

Distributed in Australia by Simon and Schuster Australia, in Canada by Ten Speed Press Canada, in New Zealand by Tandem Press, in South Africa by Real Books, and in the United Kingdom and Europe by Airlift Books.

Cover design by Catherine Jacobes
All photos copyright © 1999 by Dana Holyfield
Interior design by Jeff Brandenburg, ImageComp

Library of Congress Cataloging-in-Publication Data on file with the publisher.

First printing, 1999
Printed in the United States of America

1 2 3 4 5 6 7 8 9 10 — 03 02 01 00 99

Contents

Introduction

Now, if y'all are slap in the middle of a big city where most people have never tasted a mudbug, Gator Stew, or Smothered Frog Legs in their whole lives, it's high time you met the River People. Read this here cookbook and learn how to hunt, catch, cook, and serve up a whole mess of scrumptious fixin's at your next supper party. I'm also going to teach you how to toss up some fancy side dishes like Coonass Coleslaw, Swamped Pork'n'Beans, and Fried Dill Pickles, and to top off the evening with a taste of desserts like Wanda's Whiskey Cake. I guarantee that you will impress the heck out of your friends with the uniquely delicious swamp recipes contrived by the River People, because there is no other place on the good Lord's green earth that can season critters like we do. So roll up yer sleeves and enjoy!

CHAPTER ONE

Wild Game and Swamp Critters

A Louisiana Saturday Night on the River

Just about everybody with access to a boat makes the rounds from one camp to the other. Most of the action happens at Swampman Dan's camp, sitting on the river bank along the West Pearl—a recognized landmark with a cluster of empty whiskey bottle chimes dangling from fishing line off the cypress tree out front. Some have called it "a work of art." During the summer, Swampman Dan's camp is like a twenty-four-hour drive-thru, people stopping for a cold beer and something to eat. Except these folks show up by boat, and instead of finding a quarter pounder on the grill, they find some kind of wild animal over the fire or a picnic table covered with swamp mudbugs. They might even find something they have never eaten before but will try it just for the heck of it. When night falls, the party starts. The River People hoot and holler and eat till they feel like a bunch of stuffed hogs. After their bellies get full, they lounge around, talking about how many fish so-and-so caught on their trot line, whose old lady kicked them out of the house for not coming off the river the night before, and whose turn it is to make another beer run. When the night winds down, some River People head off to their houseboats or their camps around the bend, or some just stay at Mr. Dan's camp in one of the twelve bunk beds and then get woken up Sunday about noon when the ones that left come back to pick up where they left off. Then they make homemade biscuits and strong coffee and wish they hadn't drank so much the night before.

Alligator Rodeo in Honey Island Swamp

I knew a few swamp cowboys who took great pride in roping gators the way John Wayne roped cattle. They tied their claws to their tails before the tail whipped around and knocked them over.

Wrestling gators was a sport to swamp cowboys looking for some action in the evening. It beat the heck out of getting scolded by their old ladies or their mamas for hanging out in a barroom. When they were in the swamp with a bunch of good old boys, she didn't have anything to worry about—except her man getting eaten by a gator. After the swamp cowboys got a gator and skinned it, they cut it up for the frying pan, froze some for later, and gave the rest to friends and family who appreciated the trouble. These days it's a federal offense to get caught with a gator when it's not in season. Back when I was a kid, we didn't consider gators an endangered species. If we kept our eyes open, we could easily find a few sunning on a big log not even bothered by us long as we kept our distance. Although we did lose a few dogs now and then, the ones that swam across the river to hunt. We found one's tail once and buried it out of respect. He was a good dog.

The Alligator Man's Gator Stew

½ cup vegetable oil
8 cups alligator meat, cubed ½ inch thick
½ cup chopped onions
½ cup chopped green onions
½ cup chopped bell peppers
½ cup chopped celery
2 tablespoons minced parsley
1 (10-ounce) can tomatoes
Dash of cayenne pepper
Salt and black pepper to taste

Put the oil in a large saucepan over medium heat and add the alligator meat. Cook until brown. Then add the chopped vegetables, parsley, tomatoes, cayenne pepper, salt, and black pepper. Cover the pot and cook for 30 to 40 minutes, stirring occasionally.

Swamp Cowboy's Alligator Poorboys

Terral says, "When alligators are in season, get you a four- or five-footer, skin its tail, then cut it up in itty-bitty pieces, 'bout the size of stew meat. Then make your batter."

Oil for deep frying
1 cup yellow cornmeal
1 cup white flour
1 teaspoon salt
1 teaspoon pepper
Tony Chachere's Creole Seasoning to taste
2 cups alligator meat, cubed
French bread

Put the 3 to 4 inches of oil in a skillet over high heat.

In a mixing bowl, combine the cornmeal, flour, salt, pepper, and Tony Chachere's Creole Seasoning. Poor the mixture into a paper bag. Drop the meat into the bag a few pieces at a time. Shake the bag until the meat is coated, then drop the meat into the oil.

Deep-fry until golden brown, then transfer to a paper towel to cool. Put the alligator meat on the French bread and dress with lettuce, tomato, ketchup, mayonnaise, and tartar sauce and serve.

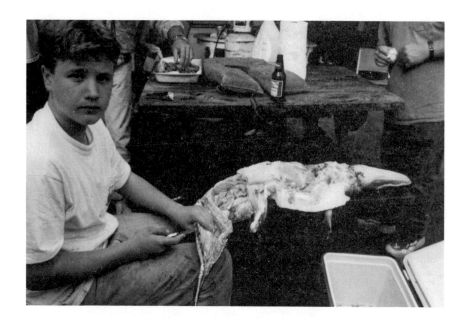

Alligator Meatballs

2 pounds alligator meat,
  ground
1 egg
1 teaspoon cayenne pepper
¼ cup whole milk
½ cup bread crumbs
2 teaspoons salt

½ teaspoon black pepper
2 tablespoons chopped parsley
½ cup green onions, chopped
Juice of 1 lemon
1 cup white flour
1 cup cornmeal
Vegetable oil for frying

In a large mixing bowl, combine the alligator with the egg, cayenne pepper, milk, bread crumbs, salt, black pepper, parsley, green onions, and lemon juice. Form into small meatballs. In another bowl, mix the flour and cornmeal. Roll the alligator meatballs in the mixture.

Put about ½ inch of oil in a skillet. Add the meatballs and fry until brown. Serve the meatballs on French bread or over pasta and rice.

Gator Sauce Piquante

½ cup flour
1 cup vegetable oil
1 large white onion, chopped
1 clove garlic, chopped
1 (14-ounce) can tomato sauce
3 cups water
1 (14-ounce) can stewed tomatoes

1 bell pepper, chopped
1 pound alligator meat,
  chopped in tiny pieces
Salt and pepper to taste
½ cup green onion tops,
  chopped

Make a roux with the flour and oil until medium brown (see below). Add the white onion to the roux and cook 10 minutes longer, until the onion is softened.

Add the garlic, tomato sauce, water, tomatoes, and bell pepper. Cook over low heat for 30 minutes. Add the gator meat, salt and pepper, and green onions. Cook 30 to 45 minutes, until meat is tender.

Roux

Roux is a thick Cajun gravy used in stews, sauces, and gumbos—or even served by itself over white rice. It is generally made with flour, oil, and sometimes butter. To make roux, heat up your oil, and slowly stir in the flour. Continue stirring over medium heat until browned. Lower the heat and continue stirring, cooking until the mixture reaches the desired color. The darker the color, the more intense the flavor. Proportions of flour and oil will vary in this book from recipe to recipe, but you'll find the basic cooking instructions here.

Let's Go Froggin'

I didn't know what to expect, but I knew to expect something interesting. There we were in the middle of the moonlit swamp, floating silently on the water listening for a croaker. After a while you can tell the difference between a gator and a bullfrog. While my brother, Mark, steered the boat, our friend Scott shined a spotlight along the dark, still water. We saw a big one. It must have been a two-pounder. The bullfrog froze in the spotlight like a possum does in the headlights. I thought Scott was going to throw a net on it or something, but lo and behold he lunged and grabbed it with both his hands! Within minutes he saw another one. I thought he would grab that one too, but he whacked it on the head with the boat paddle. Then he grabbed the unconscious bullfrog, slung it into the boat by my feet, and told me to put it in the sack with the other one. After we caught a dozen or so, we came across one about the size of a coon. This time there was no grabbing or whacking. Mark aimed his shotgun and yelled, "Watch out!" I ducked and he fired, killing the frog and almost killing me with a heart attack. That bullfrog sank full of buckshot, and I had had about enough frogging for one evening, so I told the boys to take me back to dry land. And they did. And then they informed me that I had to cook the frog legs.

They skinned the frogs for me and cut the legs off, and then Mark battered them up. I did my part by throwing them into the hot grease. Mark said, "Don't worry 'bout 'em jumpin' around in the pan. It's just the nerves."

I thought he was kidding—till one of the frog legs leaped right out the pan and hit the floor. I almost fainted right then and there, but I couldn't let the boys see me do that or I'd never hear the end of it, so I pulled myself together and rinsed the frog leg off, battered it again, threw it back into the grease, and waited for it to stop kicking around.

To keep this from happening you can clip the tendon in the knee after you have skinned the frog and cut off the legs.

Mark's Hoppin' Frog Legs

2 cups yellow cornmeal
1 cup flour
1 teaspoon salt
Pepper to taste

1 teaspoon Tony Chachere's
   Creole Seasoning
12 frogs
½ gallon vegetable oil

Combine the cornmeal, flour, salt, pepper, and Tony Chachere's Creole Seasoning in a large mixing bowl.

Skin the frogs, cut off their legs, and clip the nerve if you don't want them to jump around in the pot.

Coat the frog legs in the batter. Heat the oil in a deep pot, add the frog legs, and deep-fry till golden brown, about 10 minutes. Serve with ketchup and horseradish.

Porter's Slough Smothered Frog Legs

2 tablespoons butter
6 pairs of frog legs from
   Porter's Slough
Salt and pepper to taste
4 white onions, chopped
6 tomatoes, chopped

1 bay leaf
1 sprig thyme
¼ cup chopped parsley
1 clove garlic, minced
4 bell peppers, finely chopped
1 cup water

Melt the butter in a skillet. Add the frog legs and cook till golden brown. Then add salt, pepper, and the onions. Cook until the onions start to brown. Add the tomatoes, bay leaf, thyme, parsley, and garlic. Cover and cook for 30 minutes.

Then add the bell peppers and water. Continue cooking 45 minutes to 1 hour, till the frog legs are tender.

The Annual Squirrel Hunting Contest

The first weekend of squirrel season a hunting contest is held at Swampman Dan's camp. Prior to that weekend, all the hunters get together and put twenty dollars each in a jar. Then whoever is in charge of the money goes shopping for some nice prizes—an assortment of hunting rifles, fishing rods, and maybe an outboard motor, depending how many hunters entered.

The contestants' names are placed on a scoreboard. Friday night women aren't allowed at the camp because the men get together to discuss the hunt and get drunk as fools. Saturday morning the men who aren't too hung over head into the swamp with their rifles and the women come out to see who wins.

Around 10 A.M., the hunters start coming back. Some have a couple of squirrels, some have none, some come back with something besides a squirrel—they just couldn't resist. Then there are those who don't come back at all, but somebody eventually finds them

passed out by a cypress tree. When everybody returns from the swamp and the contest is over, the party continues on into the night.

At the 1997 Annual Squirrel Hunt, the winners were Steve Williams, Johnny Pelas, Charlie Vaughan, and Scott Bond. After they got their prizes, a hog was thrown on the grill. Jo Wilson, a member of the Bogue Chitto Choo Choo Freedom Floaters, skinned 104 donated squirrels all by himself, and Charlie Vaughan and Steve Williams made a squirrel stew with them. Bobby Commeaux's Country Music Band arrived by boat to play music at nightfall. Another hundred or so people showed up by boat, Red Dog howled a little tune, and everybody danced in the moonlight.

Charlie and Steve's Tree Rat Stew

First you'll need about 100 tree rats (otherwise known as squirrels). If you're lucky, someone else will skin them for you. Then you cut up a bunch of onions, carrots, celery, bell peppers, garlic, and whatever else you feel like putting in the stew. Set that aside while you get your water ready in a big pot. Season it with salt, pepper, thyme, and cayenne. Put your squirrels in the water. Make a lot of roux (see page 6). When the squirrels get tender, put the roux in the pot. Add a couple cans of tomato paste and your vegetables. Stir occasionally, and when nobody is looking, scoop the squirrel hair out of the foam on top. Cook the stew till the squirrel meat comes off the bone. Serve over rice. (This recipe served over 150 people at last year's Annual Squirrel Hunt. To make it at home, use fewer squirrels—about 8—and modify other ingredients roughly in proportion).

Roasted Squirrel

½ pound smoked bacon, cubed
4 squirrels, skinned, cleaned, and cut into small pieces
2 onions, chopped
1 stalk celery, chopped

About 4 cups chicken broth
Salt to taste
Pinch of thyme
½ teaspoon cayenne pepper

Brown the bacon in a large saucepan and set aside. Then brown the squirrel in the bacon grease. Set that aside.

Add the onions and celery to the oil and sauté for 2 minutes. Then add the squirrel meat, bacon, and just enough chicken broth to cover the bottom of the pan. Add the salt, thyme, and cayenne pepper, cover, and cook over low heat. Add more broth as needed. Cook about 1 hour, until the squirrel meat is tender.

Rabbit in Tomato Gravy

½ cup vegetable oil
1 large rabbit, skinned, cleaned, and cut up
1 large onion, chopped
1 bunch green onions, chopped
1 pack fresh mushrooms, sliced

5 cloves garlic
1 (14-ounce) can stewed tomatoes
1 tablespoon tomato sauce
⅓ cup water
1 teaspoon parsley

Brown the rabbit in the oil. Remove and set aside. Sauté the onion, green onions, mushrooms, and garlic. Add the stewed tomatoes, tomato sauce, and the water and cook until the sauce thickens. Then add the rabbit and cook about 1 hour, until tender. Add the parsley and serve over rice.

Barbara's Rabbit and Gravy

1 large rabbit, cleaned and
 cut into small pieces
1 tablespoon bacon grease
1 yellow onion, chopped
2 bunches green onions,
 chopped

3 cloves garlic, chopped
½ tablespoon Tony Chachere's
 Creole Seasoning
4 cups cooked white rice

In a large skillet, brown the rabbit in the bacon grease. Reduce the heat and add the onion, green onions, garlic, and Tony Chachere's Creole Seasoning. Stir, cover, and simmer for about 45 minutes, stirring occasionally. Serve over rice or on bread.

Cousin Donald's Wild Boar Dog Run

A wild boar is a wild hog in case you didn't already know—except they're uglier than sin. They kind of look like an animal that dug its way up from hell, with long tusks coming out of their snouts and long, wiry hair. They're mean as hell, too. A dog run is when a hunter takes his pit bulls out to the swampy marsh and lets them cut loose on a big boar. It's supposedly a big thrill to hunters like Donald, who have to keep up with their dogs as they tear through the swampland after the wild boar. When the dogs corner the boar, the hunter kills it if it looks like one he wants to eat.

If you're planning on taking a stroll on foot through the swampland, you're liable to come across a wild boar sooner or later. If you don't have a gun handy, you better run fast and climb the nearest tree.

Preparing Wild Boar for Eating

First kill a wild boar, hang it upside down from a backhoe or tree or something, and then skin it and clean it out. You'll need your skill saw to cut it up. If you can't stomach that, or perhaps ain't good with a saw, send it to your local meat market and they'll do it for you. Have them cut it into sections and bag them separately. You can also have them make sausage, pork roast, bacon, and other tasty treats. Freeze your meat till you are ready to cook it.

Hog Tied and Silly Pork Roast

1 large pork roast
2 bulbs garlic, sliced
1 large onion, sliced
1 large bell pepper, sliced
Tony Chachere's Creole
   Seasoning

Salt and pepper to taste
1 bunch green onions
1 pack bacon

Make deep holes in the pork roast with a knife. Put the garlic, onion, and bell pepper slices in the holes.

Sprinkle the roast with Tony Chachere's Creole Seasoning and salt and pepper. Lay the green onions on the roast and wrap the roast and green onions with the bacon slices.

Wrap the entire thing with foil and cook it in the smoker for several hours till it's done.

West Pearl Boudin

2 pounds wild boar meat
1½ pounds wild boar liver
Salt and pepper to taste
1 large onion, chopped
2 bunches green onions,
   chopped

1 bunch parsley, chopped
6 cups cooked white rice
Sausage casings, soaked
   in cold water

Cook the wild boar meat, liver, and salt and pepper in enough boiling water to cover the meat until the meat falls apart, about 45 minutes. Remove the meat and reserve some of the broth.

Mix the meat, onion, green onions, and parsley (reserving about ½ cup of green onion and parsley) and grind.

Combine the ground wild boar meat mixture with the remaining green onions and parsley, rice, and enough broth to make a moist dressing.

Stuff the dressing into the sausage casings using a sausage stuffer and serve.

Deer Sausage and Wild Boar Sausage Jambalaya

2 tablespoons butter or oleo
1 cup chopped onions
½ cup chopped celery
¼ cup chopped bell pepper
3 cloves garlic, minced
1½ pounds deer sausage, sliced and browned
1 pound wild boar sausage, sliced and browned
2 teaspoons monosodium glutamate

½ teaspoon cayenne pepper
1 tablespoon Worcestershire sauce
½ teaspoon chili powder
½ teaspoon thyme
1½ cups uncooked long-grain rice
1 cup chopped baked ham
3 cups beef stock, or 3 bouillon cubes dissolved in 3 cups water

Melt the butter in a large saucepan over medium heat. Add the onions, celery, bell pepper, and garlic and cook until browned.

Then add the deer and boar sausage, monosodium glutamate, cayenne pepper, Worcestershire sauce, chili powder, and thyme. Mix well and cook 20 minutes on low heat, stirring occasionally.

Add the rice and baked ham and cook 5 minutes more over medium heat. Stir in the beef stock. Bring to a boil and cook uncovered for about 10 minutes more, until liquid is absorbed and rice is cooked.

The Big Deer Hunt

This is another important event among hunters and wives who have to put up with the endless chatter that leads up to the big opening day of deer season. These women have learned to deal with the fact that they don't see their men for a few days when the quest is on. Besides the deer meat, a goal of these proud hunters is to get a suitable rack (with the head) that they can mount and hang over the fireplace to stare at the company.

Swampman Dan's Deer Meat Chili

3 pounds hamburger meat
5 pounds ground deer meat

1 (3-ounce) pack 7-Alarm Chili Mix

First, cook the hamburger meat until it's about halfway done. Drain the grease. Add the deer meat and 7-Alarm Chili Mix and simmer 45 minutes, stirring every 5 minutes. Serve with crackers.

Deer Hunters' Special Deer Roast

For extra flavor, wrap the deer roast with strips of bacon and shove garlic cloves in it. Salt and pepper it, shake some Worcestershire sauce on it, then wrap the hunk of meat with aluminum foil and roast it on the grill for 2 to 3 hours. If it's not done, keep cooking it.

Fried Deer Meat

Vegetable oil for frying
2 cups white flour
Salt and pepper to taste
1 teaspoon Tony Chachere's
   Creole Seasoning

12 thin slices of deer meat,
   about the size of pork chops

Heat ½ inch oil in a skillet over medium-high heat. Combine the flour and seasonings in a mixing bowl. Roll the deer meat in the flour mixture until it's evenly coated. Throw the meat in the hot oil and cook till it's tender, about 3 minutes. Serve on French bread with ketchup, or over rice with vegetables.

Deer Stew

½ cup vegetable oil
2 pounds deer meat, cubed
1 cup chopped bell pepper
½ cup chopped celery
¼ cup chopped parsley
1 cup chopped onions
Salt, pepper, and garlic
   powder to taste

2 (14-ounce) cans cream of
   mushroom soup
1 cup burgundy wine
3 cups chopped carrots
3 cups chopped potatoes

Heat the oil in a cast-iron skillet over medium heat. Add the stew meat and cook until browned, about 15 minutes. Add the bell pepper, celery, parsley, onions, salt and pepper, garlic powder, soup, wine, carrots, and potatoes. Cover and bake at 200° for no less than 8 hours.

Fifi the Huntin' Poodle

Terral is considered an outlaw to local game wardens who eagerly await the moment they can catch him red-handed. One day Terral had been hunting nutria, which are land-water mammals with grayish fur and big teeth—kind of like a beaver. He had a whole truckload when the game warden stopped him and wanted to know if he had a hunting dog with him—because it is illegal to hunt nutria without one.

Terral said, "Yes, sir, I had one."

The game warden said, "You better produce a dog in fifteen minutes or I'm gonna arrest you."

Terral thought fast and said, "Okay, follow me."

The game warden followed Terral back to the nearest friend's house that he could convince to hand over a dog. Terral jumped out his truck and said, "Wait out here and I'll get my dog."

The game warden stood outside, arms crossed, knowing Terral didn't have a dog that night. He was probably thinking he was about to make a big arrest that would be reported in the newspaper the next morning. When the door opened, Terral stepped out with Fifi, a fluffy black poodle with red ribbons on her ears and red toenail polish. "Here she is," Terral said, with a straight face.

The game warden's jaw dropped, he was speechless—and mad. "That there poodle with the red ribbons on her ears ain't rounded up all them nutria."

"She most certainly did. Fifi is one of the best nutria hunting dogs I ever owned."

"Then how come she ain't got no mud on her paws?" The game warden wondered.

About that time, Terral's good buddy stepped outside and said, "'Cauz she just had a bath. Fifi hates to get dirty."

The game warden tried to keep his cool, "I think I'm gonna have to make a call 'bout this."

"Look, you said to produce a dog and I did," Terral said.

The game warden knew he was outnumbered and couldn't prove a thing, so he got back in his truck and said, "Next time, y'all gonna have to prove that durn poodle can hunt."

When the game warden drove away, Terral cracked up and handed Fifi over to her rightful owner.

Terral's Barbecued Nutria

Skin and clean a nutria and chop the meat into cubes. Marinate in picante sauce for a few hours. Put the meat on skewers and brush with a mixture of 1 cup barbecue sauce, 1 teaspoon salt, 1 teaspoon pepper, and 1 teaspoon Tony Chachere's Creole Seasoning. Throw the skewers on the grill and cook, turning occasionally, for about 1 hour, or until the meat is tender but cooked through.

Uncle Dave's Southern Yankee BBQ Chicken

2 or 3 whole chickens,
   plucked and cleaned
2 (14-ounce) cans cream
   of mushroom soup
2 (14-ounce) cans cream
   of celery soup

1 bunch celery, chopped
15 mushrooms, sliced
Salt and pepper to taste

Put the chickens in a deep baking pan and pour the cream of mushroom and cream of celery soup over them. Add the celery, mushrooms, and salt and pepper. Stir and cook for about 1 hour.

Swampman Dan's Drunken Chicken

If I hadn't seen it with my own eyes, I wouldn't have believed it. So I took a picture so you'd believe it too (see the color photo section). Swampman Dan (my daddy) cooks drunken chicken. Here's how he does it: The first thing you need is a couple of chickens. Then get a six-pack of beer. For each chicken, cut the top off one of the cans. Leave half of the beer in the can—drink the other half. Pour a teaspoon each of salt and pepper in the can with the beer. Add 1 teaspoon Worcestershire sauce, 2 tablespoons liquid crab boil, and a teaspoon of Tony Chachere's Creole Seasoning. Then shove the can into the whole chicken. Set it up on the grill and cover. Let it cook till the chicken "gets drunk," about 1 hour.

CHAPTER TWO

Gone Fishin'

Denty Crawford's Swampland Villa

Denty's swamp hideaway is another happening stop for the River People and the few welcomed outsiders who can get there by boat or vehicle. Denty built the grounds up like a fortress. He's landscaped it with driftwood, Christmas lights year 'round, and moss-draped cypress trees. The swamp is his backyard. People come from all over the world to party at Denty's. But only when the fifteen-foot-high gate is open. When it's not, that means go away for a while—but not too long. Between forty and fifty people stop by during a weekend gala. At times there have been a hundred or more. If you're new, you'll be told to watch out for the rabbits, and don't worry about getting attacked by pet wild boar, and don't stick your finger in the parrots' cage because they might bite. Other than that, you're told to just have fun. There are usually crawfish boiling and catfish frying. Denty's got a secret recipe for his fried catfish, and he's sharing it with us.

Denty Crawford's Fried Catfish

The trick is to fillet the fish in quarter-inch slabs and soak them all day in the batter, or if I don't have all day, I soak them at least 4 hours.

The first thing you need to make the batter is a medium-sized squirt bottle of mustard. Squirt the whole thing in a bucket or bowl. Then squeeze half a lemon into the mustard. Add about a teaspoon of cayenne pepper, some garlic powder, a little cornmeal, and about a cup of water—enough to make it soupy. Put a little bit of salt in, and mix it up. Then for the dry batter, I get a plate of cornmeal, about a teaspoon of cayenne pepper, and garlic powder, salt, and pepper to taste, and mix it around. Another thing I do is put muffin mix in the batter to make it sweet tasting. And maybe some Zatarain's Spicy Fish Fry Seasoning if I feel like it. The grease has to be about 3 inches deep and good and hot before you fry them. I use a colander to shake off the excess cornmeal batter. Another secret is to cook one piece of fish first and taste it before cooking the rest. If you want a real pretty piece of cooked fish, don't roll it in the corn-meal batter too long, because the cornmeal will get clumpy and fall off. Throw a fillet in the pot. It'll come up to the top, but that does-n't mean it's ready. Turn it a few times, wait till it turns golden brown, then remove it. Let it cool down on a towel. (I don't use paper towels—I use a real towel.) After it's cooled a bit, I taste it to see if it's missing something, or if it's too spicy or too salty. Then I can adjust the seasoning before I make the rest. Once you get the taste right, cook a handful at a time. It'll take you a few tries to get it right. And everybody does it differently, but everybody who eats my fried fish comes back for more.

Snapper Turtle Soup

2½ pounds turtle meat, cut into small pieces
1 teaspoon salt
1 teaspoon pepper
4 tablespoons vegetable oil
3 tablespoons flour
2 large onions, chopped
1 cup chopped celery
½ cup chopped bell peppers
2 cloves garlic, minced
1½ (14-ounce) cans tomato sauce
1 cup plus 2 quarts water
1 lemon, sliced
4 bay leaves
1 teaspoon parsley
½ cup sherry
1 tablespoon Worcestershire sauce
4 hard-boiled eggs, sliced
Paprika for garnish

Season the turtle meat with salt and pepper. Put the oil in a large saucepan over medium heat, add the turtle meat, and cook till browned. Remove the meat from the pan. Next add the flour, browning slowly till golden.

Then add the onions, celery, bell peppers, and garlic and cook till tender, about 10 minutes.

Return the turtle meat to the pot and add the tomato sauce and 1 cup of water. Cook about 30 minutes.

Then add the lemon, bay leaves, and 2 quarts of water. Simmer the soup for 1 hour, or till the soup has reduced to the desired thickness.

Stir in the parsley, sherry, and Worcestershire sauce. Place slices of hard-boiled eggs into the soup. Sprinkle with paprika.

Barbara's Needle-Nose Gar

1 needle-nose gar, cleaned
  and cut up
Tony Chachere's Creole
  Seasoning

1 (16-ounce) bottle yellow
  mustard
Tony Chachere's Fish Fry
Vegetable oil for deep-frying

Sprinkle the gar with Tony Chachere's Creole Seasoning, then soak it in the mustard for 4 hours. Roll it in Tony Chachere's Fish Fry. Deep-fry it in hot oil till it's golden brown.

Fisherman's Stuffed Flounder

2 large flounders, cleaned
Salt and pepper to taste
Tony Chachere's Creole
  Seasoning to taste
1 stick butter
1 bunch green onions,
  finely chopped

1 bell pepper, chopped
8 ounces cream cheese
1 cup cooked crab meat
Juice of 1 lemon

Slice the flounders along the main bone. Season inside and out with salt and pepper and Tony Chachere's Creole Seasoning. Melt half the stick of butter in a large skillet and sauté the green onions and bell pepper for about 15 minutes. Add the cream cheese and continue sautéing until melted. Add the crab meat and mix well. Stuff the flounders with the cream cheese and crab meat mixture. Melt the remaining butter in the skillet, add the lemon juice, and season to taste with more salt and pepper and Tony Chachere's Creole Seasoning. Baste the stuffed flounders with the melted butter and bake at 350° for 45 minutes.

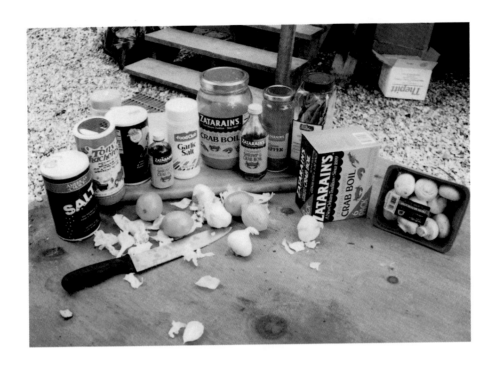

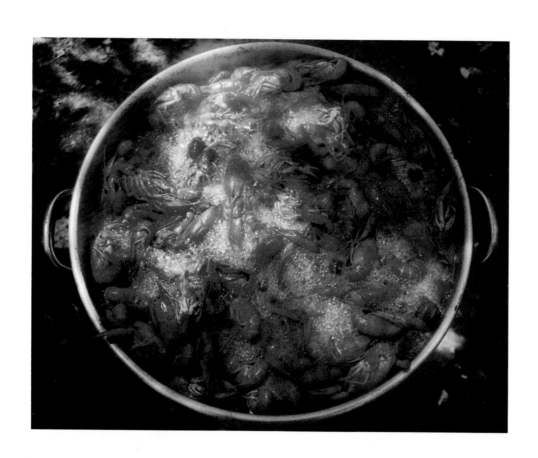

Joan's Boiled Oysters

1 sack oysters in shells
1 pot of water that was used to boil crawfish (or use "ready
    mix" for crawfish/crab boil with plain water)

Boil the oysters in the water until the shells crack open. Dip them
out of the pot, let them cool, and eat them right out of the shells.

Smokey's Damn Good Oysters

1 pint oysters   1 (8-ounce) jar sweet relish
1 pound bacon   Butter to top

Place the oysters in a deep baking pan. Wrap a strip of bacon
around each oyster. Top each with a touch of sweet relish. Then dot
all with butter. Bake at 350° for about 15 minutes, or until the bacon
is cooked. Drain excess grease and serve.

Oyster and Broccoli Goo-lash

2 bunches broccoli,
   chopped into small pieces
3 cups cooked white rice
1 pint oysters, drained
¾ cup sour cream
2 tablespoons ketchup
¼ cup whole milk
2 teaspoons sherry

2 teaspoons lemon juice
1 teaspoon cream horseradish
1½ teaspoons Worcestershire
   sauce
8 drops hot pepper sauce
1½ teaspoons onion salt
½ cup buttered bread crumbs

Steam the broccoli and toss it lightly with the cooked rice. Spoon the mixture into a greased casserole dish. Arrange the oysters on top of the rice mixture.

Combine the remaining ingredients, except the bread crumbs, and pour everything over the oysters. Sprinkle with the bread crumbs.

Bake at 350° for 20 minutes.

Mrs. Carol's Oyster Stew

2 tablespoons butter
½ cup minced celery
Dash of Worcestershire sauce
2 dozen oysters

2 cups whole milk
2 cups light cream
Salt and pepper to taste
Paprika for garnish

Heat the butter in a saucepan over medium heat. Add the celery and sauté until tender. Add the Worcestershire sauce and oysters with their liquid. Heat slowly for about 3 minutes, until the oysters begin to curl. Add the milk, cream, salt, and pepper. Heat just to boiling—but do not boil. Garnish with paprika.

Indian Village Catfish Lounge

The Catfish Lounge is another happening hangout for the River People when they want something different to do than lounge around the camp listening to stories. Here, they can hang out in an air-conditioned watering hole and listen to the same stories, and maybe some new ones from outsiders. When they come by boat, they look like a fleet of rowdy coonasses drifting down the Pearl River ready for a good time. When they enter the Catfish Lounge, there's a whole lot of handshaking as if it's been a long time—a week is considered a good stretch in Louisiana. The jukebox gets pumped with quarters, unless Box Car Billie and Mark Holyfield bring their guitars and are in the mood to sing, which is usually the case. If it's one of these nights, everybody gathers in the back room by the big dance floor in case somebody is in the mood to do the alligator crawl—that's a dance. The ones who can play music and sing, or try to sing, take turns entertaining the crowd. The Catfish Lounge serves Cajun food and a damn good Bloody Mary, among other good drinks. So y'all come on by and have some fun. If you come by vehicle, just drive down old I-90 and take a left on Indian Village Road towards the Pearl River. Go all the way to the end. It's the building on the right, across from the building on the left (the Swamp Monster Tour Gift Shop). If you come by boat, just dock at the Indian Village Boat Landing. If you get lost, call (504) 649-5778.

Cole's Cheatin' Shrimp Jambalaya

¼ cup vegetable oil
1 large onion, chopped
1½ gallons spaghetti sauce
1 teaspoon salt
1 teaspoon white pepper
1 teaspoon black pepper

1 teaspoon cayenne pepper
2 teaspoons Italian seasoning
½ teaspoon basil
5 pounds peeled shrimp
2½ gallons cooked rice

Put the oil in a large pot and heat. Add the onions and sauté until they are clear. Then add the spaghetti sauce and all other ingredients except the shrimp and rice. Let it come to a light boil, then turn down the heat and simmer for 30 minutes, stirring to keep it from sticking. Then add the shrimp. Cook and stir for another 15 minutes. Add the sauce to the rice till most of the liquid is absorbed.

Nelwyn's B-B-Q Shrimp

Soak 5 pounds of shrimp, with the heads still on, in salty ice water for 2 hours.

Brown 1 stick of butter in a saucepan over medium heat for about 5 minutes. Then add 3 more sticks of butter to the browned butter and melt. Stir in 1 tablespoon cayenne pepper, 1 tablespoon black pepper, 1 teaspoon Tabasco sauce, 1 tablespoon Worcestershire sauce, 1 bulb chopped garlic, and a 7-ounce can of Minute Maid frozen lemon juice.

Add the shrimp to the sauce and bring to a boil. Cover, reduce the heat, and let sit for 5 minutes. Remove from the heat and serve with French bread.

Rusty's Mudbug Secret Recipe

Boilin' Mudbugs

I asked the River People to give up their secret recipe for boiling crawfish (we call them mudbugs in the swamp). They wanted to know why it was a secret, because everybody they know already knows how. I explained that I was writing a cookbook for people all over the country. They got defensive, not liking the idea of out-siders knowing their business. Then I told them they'd be famous. There was a moment of silence while they thought it over, then they volunteered Rusty to do the talking since he is an authority on boiling crawfish. So I grabbed my pen and paper and waited for Rusty to launch into his recipe. Instead, he explained, "I can't just tell you how I do it, 'cause I don't go by no particular recipe. You're just gonna have to watch what I do."

Before you can get started, you have to catch a sack of mudbugs (about 40 or 50 pounds). Or you could do it the easy way and go to town and buy some live ones (it's best to keep crawfish alive till you throw them in the pot). Don't cover them with water till you boil them because they'll die fast. If you are bringing the sack home from the market, keep it tied tight so they don't crawl around and pinch each other, and be easy with the sack so they don't get smushed. (Note: Crawfish are in season in the spring, about March through June.)

And if you can't catch any or buy any where you live, I know some seafood places that can Fed-Ex everything you need overnight on dry ice. (Try New Orleans Over Night, Inc. Mail-order seafood and Cajun cuisine, "From the Bayou to You!" (800) NU-AWLINS, www.nuawlins.com.)

Cooking Utensils

You will need a real big pot (60 quarts) for 40 to 50 pounds, and it's a darn shame to boil anything less than that. You'll need a butane burner, too (5-gallon butane burner and bottle). If you don't have your own, you can rent one. You will also need a boat paddle for stirring. Don't bother with forks or spoons, unless somebody is bringing potato salad or coleslaw.

Purging Mudbugs

It's important to purge the mudbugs before you boil them. Put the crawfish in an ice chest or washtub or something else big enough to hold them all. Rinse them real good two or three times, then fill the tub with water till they're covered. Dump in half a box of salt, and let them sit for about 25 minutes. The salt will make them spit up all that mud. After that, you'll need to drain them and rinse them again a couple times.

Set Up

Spread lots of newspapers on top of your picnic table about five or six sheets thick (newspaper soaks up the juice). Or you can use an old bed sheet—one that you aren't planning to sleep on again. If you don't have a picnic table, you can set up plywood on two saw horses, or use a canoe or old boat with a hole cut in the bottom with a bucket underneath to catch the heads and tails, like the one Denty's got in his yard.

Guests

The next thing you'll need is a crowd. About ten to twenty folks will do to start. Once word gets out how good you boil crawfish, the crowd will gather like mosquitoes on a humid night. Make sure

you don't invite anybody who's allergic to shellfish or iodine. That puts a real damper on things.

Ingredients and Seasonings

8-ounce bottle of liquid crab boil. Pour the whole thing in.

A big box of Zatarain's crab boil. If you're boiling a 40- to 50-pound sack, use 4 to 6 bags of crab boil. (You're not supposed to tear the bags open, but some folks do.)

Salt. Use a whole box, and don't worry about anybody with high blood pressure. If they're that sick, then they should have stayed home.

Cayenne pepper. Pour in the whole bottle (8 ounces) but use your own judgment, depending on how many pounds you're boiling and how hot you like them.

Lemons. Get about 6. Cut them in half, squeeze the juice into the water, then drop them in the pot.

Onions. A sack of small onions (about a dozen), skins and all. Or if they're large ones, cut them in half.

Garlic. Use a whole sack and don't worry about peeling them. I always cut a couple bulbs down the middle to let the flavor get out, but you don't have to.

Corn on the cob. It's not a seasoning, but it adds something extra to eat. Put in about a dozen peeled cobs.

Potatoes. Potatoes aren't a seasoning either, but they soak up the seasonings pretty well. Get a sack of new potatoes and just drop them in whole. If you're using big ones, cut them into quarters.

Mushrooms. Throw in a carton or so of mushrooms if you feel like it.

Anything else you want. People are throwing in all kinds of stuff these days, like sausage, roast, chicken, gizzards, carrots, bell peppers, and whatever else they like to eat.

Water. 6 gallons to a 40-pound sack. That should fill the pot one-third of the way.

Music. These events need a good-time environment—if you've got enough money, hire a band to set up in your backyard.

Gossip. A very important detail. Don't forget to gossip about all the times the shit hit the fan.

(Note: If you want the easier way to boil mudbugs, you can order a "ready mix" when you order the crawfish. The seasonings come already mixed up in a bucket. Everything's there but the vegetables. See page 90 for ordering information.

How Long Should You Boil Mudbugs

Put your seasonings and vegetables in first. Get the water at a full boil for about 20 minutes. When the inside of the lemons come out, the water is just right. Throw the first batch of mudbugs into the boiling water. Wait till the water comes back to a boil again. When it does, boil mudbugs for 5 minutes. Then cut off the fire and let them sit for 15 to 30 minutes to soak up the seasonings. It's important to squirt the outside of the pot with the waterhose so the water in the pot cools down and don't keep cooking the crawfish. If the crawfish cook too long, they get soggy; not long enough, they're too hard. And the longer they sit, the spicier they get. You gotta let them soak for a while, or they won't taste good. So keep sampling them and make sure they don't get too spicy for you. When somebody says, "That's hot enough," take them out, and start up the next batch.

How to Eat a Mudbug

Break off the tail from the head, and suck the juice outta the head. Dig the fat out of the head with your finger, and eat that too, if you want. Then peel off the first couple of segments of the shell on the tail. Get a hold of the meat with your teeth and pinch the end of the tail with your thumb and forefinger to pull it out of its shell. It should just slide right out of there. If the black vein is still on the meat, peel it off and rub it on the newspaper or paper towel. If the crawfish claws are big enough to bother with, break them with a butter knife and eat the meat inside. You can dip the meat in cocktail sauce or eat it right out of the shell. You make better time that way. If too many people are standing next to you sucking mudbugs down like they're in a contest, you might not get your belly full if you waste time on dipping sauce. I've known grownups who have tromped over dogs and small children to get to the picnic table when the crawfish came out of the pot. So don't waste precious time.

Cleaning Up after the Boil

Roll the crawfish shells and heads in the newspaper that's already on the table. Place this into a plastic bag and get it out of there because it will stink tomorrow. But don't leave it out by the trash can or the night critters will tear open the bag and make a bigger mess than your guests did.

What to Do with Leftover Mudbugs

Save the leftover mudbugs (if there are any) for mudbug bisque, or just eat them like they are the next day. Don't keep them in the icebox more than 2 days. You can freeze them if you want to, but make sure you remove the meat from the shell before you freeze them.

Mudbug Bisque with Stuffed Crawfish Heads

20 pounds of crawfish   4 cups cooked white rice

BISQUE

6 tablespoons butter
½ cup vegetable oil
1 cup flour
2 large onions, minced
1 large bell pepper,
    finely chopped

4½ cups water
Salt to taste
1 tablespoon cayenne pepper
½ cup chopped green onions,
    tops only
½ cup chopped parsley

STUFFED CRAWFISH HEADS

¼ cup vegetable oil
½ cup white flour
2 medium onions, minced
1 large bell pepper,
    finely chopped
¾ cup water
2 teaspoons salt

1 teaspoon cayenne pepper
1½ cups bread crumbs
¼ cup chopped parsley
¼ cup chopped green onions,
    tops only
4 tablespoons butter
Extra flour

Separate the crawfish heads from the tails. Peel the tails and set them aside. Place the crawfish "fat" in a separate container and set aside. Clean 60 heads to fill with stuffing and set aside. Divide the tails and "fat" equally for bisque and for stuffing.

Bisque

Make a roux with the butter, oil, and flour (see page 6). When the roux is dark brown, add the onions and bell pepper and cook until softened, stirring often. Add half the crawfish tails and half the fat. Cook over low heat for about 20 minutes. Heat the 4½ cups water until boiling, then gradually add to the roux mixture, along with the salt and cayenne pepper, and cook for 20 minutes more. Add the green onions and parsley.

Stuffed Crawfish Heads

Make a roux with the oil and flour (see page 6). When the roux is dark brown, add the onions and bell pepper and cook until softened, stirring often. Grind the remaining crawfish tails with a food processor or meat grinder and add to the roux mixture along with the remaining fat. Simmer 15 minutes.

Add the water, salt, cayenne pepper, bread crumbs, parsley, green onions, and butter and mix well. Stuff each crawfish head with the mixture. Roll each head in flour and bake at 350° for 15 minutes.

Add the baked stuffed crawfish heads to the bisque and serve with rice.

Crawfish on a Bun

3 tablespoons vegetable oil	½ cup crawfish fat
3 tablespoons flour	¼ cup water
1 large onion, chopped	1 teaspoon cayenne pepper
½ pound crawfish tails, peeled	2 teaspoons salt

Make a roux with the vegetable oil and flour (see page 6). When the roux is dark brown, add the onion and cook till softened, about 10 minutes. Then add the crawfish, fat, water, cayenne pepper, and salt. Cook for 20 minutes. Serve on an open-face hot dog bun.

CHAPTER THREE

The Reunion of Gator and LouAnn:

Storytellin' with Recipes

Reunion of Gator and LouAnn

It seemed like any other Louisiana Saturday night: Scooter and Earl caught a bunch of mudbugs and were planning to have a boil for their friends. But they didn't know Gator gotten out of jail and was looking for LouAnn, who is Scooter's baby sister. Of course as far as Gator remembered, LouAnn wasn't so little. She carried her weight pretty good, all two-hundred pounds of it, dressing in spiked high heels, the tightest jeans she could squeeze into, and low-cut blouses that exposed mountains of cleavage. But after Gator went to jail, she lost fifty pounds or so and let her friend Mona, who was attending beauty school, bleach her brown hair as blond as she could get it without all of it falling out.

According to Gator, LouAnn was still his wife, but according to her, she'd been a free woman ever since Gator got six months in prison for robbing the Piggly Wiggly for a pint of whiskey. Mr. Bo James said he wasn't selling Gator any more liquor because he was ten sheets to the wind as it was (he had mixed whiskey with a gallon of MuskyDime wine that LouAnn left in the icebox). Mad as a hornet, Gator stumbled out to his brand-new Ford pickup truck and grabbed his twelve-gauge shotgun from the gunrack. He marched right back into the Piggly

Wiggly and said, "Mr. Bo James, gimme the durn bottle of whiskey 'fore I load somebody up with buckshot." Mr. Bo James knew Gator didn't have the heart to shoot anybody—when he was sober. But he also knew Gator could get a little out of hand when he was lit up on booze, so he gave him the bottle of whiskey and waited till he drove away to call Leroy, the local sheriff. Leroy took great pride in arresting Gator at sunrise when he found him passed out on the cypress stump at the boat dock. You see, Leroy and Gator go way back. They became buddies in junior high and stayed that way on through most of the eleventh grade—till Gator stole Leroy's girlfriend, which at that time was LouAnn.

Scooter steered the flatboat toward the riverbank, not bothering to slow down. The boat skidded up in the weeds. "Damn, Scooter! Drive us on up in the trees next time," Earl said as he staggered out the boat and tied it to a tree.

"I need a cold one," Scooter declared as he wiped the sweat off his brow. "Let's go see what Renald's got goin' on inside," Scooter said, not really needing to because Earl was headed there already, thinking Renald was pretty darn smart to open a lounge right by the boat dock. He had hunters and fishermen coming and going and sold bait and tackle in the back room, too. Earl wondered why he couldn't have thought of it first.

Scooter had to call his old lady, Roxy, nicknamed Foxy by all Scooter's buddies. He didn't mind, because he started the nickname himself. He was proud to have such a good-looking woman, that is, when she was in his line of sight. It wasn't so good when she was out running the roads with her girlfriends. "Probably stirrin' up trouble," he joked around, although he knew it was true. He called home. "Where's your mama?"

"She ain't here," Shelby told him. Shelby was Roxy's thirteen-year-old daughter from her first marriage. Shelby's twelve-year-old step-brother, Bobo, was his child.

"Where in the world did she run off to this early?" Scooter asked, looking at his watch. "It's nine-thirty in the durn mornin'."

"She went to see Mona at beauty school."

"What for?"

"To get her nails done."

"Her nails! Did she remember to get the stuff for the boil tonight?"

"How am I suppose to know what she remembered?" the teenager smarted off.

Scooter got mad and hung up. "Damn young 'uns!" He sat down and had a beer with Earl to blow off steam. It only took a minute, then he was on another subject. "Renald, you shoulda been there. We caught the heck outta them mudbugs this morning."

Then Earl chimed in, "'Bout a hundred pounds, I reckon."

Scooter added, "Renald, you come on by tonight and eat 'bout ten pounds yourself." Then Scooter invites everybody else who happened to be in the lounge.

At the beauty school, Roxy was letting Mona practice on her long fingernails.

"What's LouAnn bringing tonight?" Mona asked, carefully applying shiny red polish.

"I ain't heard from her since yesterday. She's probably with that fancy lawyer." Roxy told her.

"Wait till Gator finds out."

"She's got a few more months before she has to get worried," Roxy said.

"Nuh-uh. He's getting out of jail," Mona revealed by accident. She had been sworn to secrecy.

"Lord Jesus! When?" Roxy almost made Mona mess up her fine paint job.

"Hold still! My teacher's coming around to check this in a minute. I gotta pass so I can graduate from this godforsaken place."

"When's he getting out?" Roxy asks.

"Darrel went to get him this morning."

"Nobody told LouAnn," Roxy worried out loud.

"I tried to call her soon as Darrel walked out the door, but she wasn't home. Gator wants to surprise her anyhow," Mona admitted.

"He's gonna surprise her alright," Roxy said as she blew on her wet polish, hoping it would dry fast so she could hurry up and find LouAnn.

Scooter drug the water hose over to the bucket of mudbugs and filled it up. Then he dumped in half a box of salt to purge them.

Roxy's Iroc Z slid to a halt in the dirt driveway. Scooter gave her the eye as she carried in the groceries. "Where the hell you been, woman?"

"The grocery."

"You ain't been shoppin' all this time."

"I had errands," Roxy replied.

"Errands? That's a bunch of bullcrap."

"Gator's gettin' outta jail!"

"I know, quit avoidin' my questions."

"If you knew, why didn't you tell me?"

"I just found out."

"What if LouAnn shows up with Charles tonight?"

"Then I reckon this party oughta be entertaining. Did you get the stuff I asked you to?"

"Hold on, cowboy," Roxy answered as she fished the cayenne pepper and crab boil out the paper sack.

"You forgot the beer?" Scooter got distraught over the thought of not having enough beer for everybody to last through the night.

"No, I didn't. It's in the trunk." Roxy headed inside to the phone to try and track down LouAnn.

"Cut up the onions and corn. Or will that mess up Mona's work of art?" Scooter asked, sarcastically.

Roxy shot him a cold look, then dashed inside before he could say anything else.

LouAnn was fixing her lipstick in the rearview mirror, which happened to be the mirror in Gator's truck. She took over the payments when he went to jail, so she considered it her truck now. Her boss walked up to the truck window. "LouAnn, can you come back in tonight? Martha just called in sick."

"No sirree, I've got plans. Can't you call somebody else?"

"You're the best waitress we got for Saturday nights."

"Lord, I been workin' all night and most of the mornin'. I'm sorry but this is my night off. Get Charlene. She needs the money."

"Charlene's eight months pregnant."

"All the more reason. Them drunk fools will feel sorry for her and tip her big." LouAnn had finished that conversation. She cranked the engine and drove away from the Chicken Poop Lounge, leaving her boss in a bind.

I imagine you're wondering how in the world the barroom got that nickname. Well, it just stuck after an unusual contest the owner came up with. They drew big squares on a sheet of plywood, put numbers inside the squares, and took dollar bets on the numbers. Then they shook up a live chicken, to get her nerves good and rattled, and dropped her on the sheet of plywood. The fools who placed bets hoped that chicken would poop on their number. You wouldn't believe how many folks came out to bet on chicken shit!

LouAnn had met Charles at work. He was there to investigate a case. His client claimed the chicken was trained so it wasn't a fair game. Charles took the case only because it was his Uncle Larry's son. His

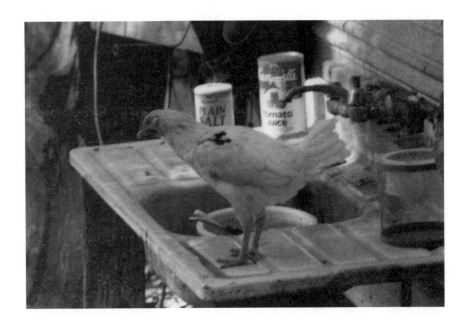

Uncle Larry paid some of his way through law school, so he felt he owed him one. But while thinking about how idiotic he was going to look to his associates in court, Charles ordered the strongest drink he could. Ever since then, he and LouAnn had been secretly meeting. Of course it wasn't much of a secret after she told Mona and Roxy, who were voted the town gossip queens. But LouAnn knew better than to take Charles home with her, because as sure as she did, the slightest breeze would carry the news right through the cracks in the cement walls of Angola and directly into Gator's cell. He'd for sure kill her when he got out. He considered it her fault he went to prison in the first place. If she wouldn't have kicked him out of the house that night for not coming off the river, putting him in a fierce state of mind, he wouldn't have held up Mr. Bo James at the Piggly Wiggly. Gator's buddies supposed he'd had grown resentful when LouAnn stopped going to visit him the month before when she met Charles. Gator refused to let any other visitors come in to talk to him—he didn't want bad news brought to him while he couldn't do anything about it from the inside. He'd rather wait till he got out and could see for hisself. And since nobody had any direct contact with Gator, nobody knew what was going on inside his head, not even his best friend Darrel, who was on his way to get him. All Darrel knew was that Gator was being let out.

Roxy dialed up LouAnn's house, which happened to be down the road from theirs, although it wasn't really a house. It was a double-wide trailer, sitting fifteen feet high on pylons because of the floods. The phone rang but there was no answer. Roxy was pacing, about to wear a hole in her linoleum.

Shelby pranced in the kitchen wearing short shorts riding as high as the moon. "What's wrong with you, Mama?"

"I got to find LouAnn."

Shelby took the Kool-Aid out the icebox and said, "LouAnn was working."

Roxy noticed the shorts. "Shelby, them shorts are too dang short."

"They ain't no shorter than the ones you wear!"

"Well, I'm a grown-up."

"So."

"Don't smart mouth me, girl or I'll wash your mouth out with soap."

Shelby disappeared outside, and Roxy went back to worrying about LouAnn.

She called the Chicken Poop Lounge and found out that LouAnn had left a couple hours earlier. She hung up, wondering where LouAnn could be, till Bobo comes in carrying a rifle. "Bobo, where you been with that gun?" Roxy asked the twelve-year-old.

"I went to kill that possum that keeps gettin' into Mrs. Betty's chicken coop."

"Did you get it?"

"Yep."

"Did you throw it in the river so it won't draw flies?"

"No, Mrs. Betty's gonna make possum stew."

Possum Stew

1 large onion, chopped	2 (14-ounce) cans stewed
2 cloves garlic, minced	tomatoes
1 bell pepper, chopped	1 bunch carrots, chopped
Salt and pepper to taste	1 possum, skinned,
3 cups water	cleaned, and cut up

Sauté the onion, garlic, and bell pepper in oil until soft, about 15 minutes. Then add salt and pepper, the water, tomatoes, and carrots. Put the possum into the pot and bring the water to a boil. Turn the heat down to medium and cook for 1 hour. Serve over rice.

———————

Just before the sun set behind the tall trees, Earl carried his steel guitar to Scooter's back yard. His brother Bubba unloaded his drum set out of his Chevy. Jimmy Jo was bringing his bass and Skeeter had his guitar and Bobo would be on keyboard. They set up on the platform that Scooter built under the magnolia tree last summer.

Colleen pulled up in her truck and stepped out of a cloud of dust like a tornado, a gallon of homemade wine in one hand and a plastic Mardi Gras cup filled with ice in the other. Colleen was Gator's older sister, who had been dating Earl for the last ten years. Earl swore he would never get married again on paper.

"Did y'all hear?" Colleen asks anyone who was paying attention.

Roxy spread newspaper out on the picnic table in the backyard. "We heard."

"What's LouAnn gonna do?" Colleen asked nervously. She was always nervous. Earl blamed it on account of her great grandma filling her baby bottle with sugar milk—strong French coffee, milk, and lots of sugar.

"LouAnn ain't nowhere to be found. I've searched high and low for her. I even called that lawyer's office, but his secretary said he was out for the day."

"Well, I hope LouAnn ain't gonna bring him tonight. I doubt Gator will handle the situation so good his first night outta prison," Colleen claims, then she has a vision that made her grin. "Hell, let Gator find out. It'll serve him right for all the times he cheated on her!"

Roxy glanced quickly at Colleen. She didn't know Gator cheated on LouAnn more than the one time he cheated with her. Of course that was almost ten years ago.

When Gator slid into Darrel's truck he didn't say anything except, "Hey, Darrel."

The ride was silent for the first fifteen minutes. Darrel knew better than to start babbling to an ex-con. It was better to let Gator start up the conversation when it felt right to him.

"I can't wait to go fishin'," Gator finally said.

Darrel cracked up. It was like a ton of bricks was lifted from him. "Yeah, they been bitin' good, too. I found a new spot."

"How's Mona?"

"She's fine. She's about to ruin me with that beauty school mumbo jumbo, wantin' to cut my hair ever two weeks and put some kinda dye on my gray. I didn't even have no gray that I could see. But, after all that I'm sure to get some."

"I was wonderin' why your hair was so durn ugly," Gator cracked.

"Wait till you see what she did to your old lady's hair," Darrel said, suddenly wishing he wouldn't have brought up LouAnn so soon. He waited for Gator to ask him about her.

"How's Scooter and the boys?" Gator asked instead.

"Same old, same old. We havin' a crawfish boil tonight." Darrel was hoping Gator wouldn't ask him anything about LouAnn because he didn't want be the one to tell him. But he knew if he didn't say something else about LouAnn, Gator would know that something was going on. "LouAnn's still workin' at the Chicken Poop Lounge," Darrel finally said to break the ice good.

Gator looked out the window, thinking about things.

Darrel changed the subject. "Your boys are growing like weeds. Dusty's almost big as Shelby. And Ollie's been going squirrel hunting with us."

That got a smile out of Gator. "Thanks for takin' time with my boys."

"They're good kids," Darrel replied.

"I've got a urge for some of them crawfish tonight." And that was all Gator said the rest of the way home.

The neighborhood regulars arrived. Most had six-packs in hand, which they dropped in the ice chest in the backyard. Earl and the boys were tuning up their instruments on the platform. Scooter had the fire going strong under the big pot of water. He threw in the ingredients and poured in a whole box of salt and half a bottle of cayenne pepper. "Hell, Scooter. Dump the whole thang in," Bubba tells him. So Scooter did.

"That's sure to make your eyes twinkle," Scooter warned everybody who saw him do it.

The women were in the kitchen gossiping. Colleen was making her famous Spicy Cajun Potato Salad, Roxy was frying hush puppies, and Mona was making Coonass Coleslaw.

Spicy Cajun Potato Salad

If you saved some potatoes from your last crawfish, shrimp, or crab boil, use them for your potato salad because they already have a spicy flavor. If you didn't save any, you can boil potatoes with a bag of crab boil and salt. After the potatoes are soft, drain them, let them cool while you make the sauce you gonna mix them in. You need a cup of mayonnaise, 3 tablespoons of mustard, some finely chopped onions, some chopped garlic, chopped green onions, chopped pickles, and whatever else you want to throw in. Shake in some hot sauce and add a pinch of black or red pepper to taste. Mix the sauce with the potatoes, and you're done.

Foxy Roxy's Hush Puppies

2 cups self-rising cornmeal
3 cloves garlic, minced
1 large white onion, chopped
1 bunch green onions, chopped (optional)
1 (14-ounce) can creamed corn (optional)
½ cup jalapeño peppers or to taste (optional)
Salt and pepper to taste
Vegetable oil for deep-frying
2 eggs
⅓ cup milk

It's important not to put in the liquid ingredients until you're ready to throw the hush puppies into the oil because your batter will get soggy. Fill a bowl with cornmeal and add your chopped garlic, onion, green onions, corn, jalapeños, salt, and pepper. Get your oil real hot (use a deep pot so the hush puppies will float to the top). Put a cup of water next to the pot so you can dip your spoon in it between each hush puppy. In other words, when you scoop up a hush puppy and drop it into the hot oil, rinse your spoon before you get the next scoop. When your oil is good and hot, add the milk and egg to your batter. Stir it well, scoop up the batter into a ball, and drop it into the oil. Put in only a couple at a time because they'll stick together if there are too many. When they float to the top, turn them a couple times till they get brown. Remove them from the oil, and put them on a paper towel to drain. Repeat till all your batter has been used.

Coonass Coleslaw

1 head green cabbage, chopped
1 head red cabbage, chopped
3 tablespoons tartar sauce
3 tablespoons mayonnaise
3 teaspoons horseradish

Hot sauce to taste
Red pepper to taste
Salt and pepper to taste
2 cups cooked shrimp or
    crawfish (or both)

Mix well and serve.

Gator walked into his double-wide and noticed that LouAnn had rearranged the furniture. He took his boots off in his easy chair, which she had covered with a pink flowery blanket. He inspected the girly material and shook his head in disgust. But he was more disgusted knowing LouAnn hadn't been home all day, because he couldn't smell the perfume she squirted on her neck every time she went to the bathroom.

Gator took off his shirt and blue jeans, got in the shower, and rinsed away the grime of prison. He noticed a black lacy pair of panties hanging on the towel rack, drying. He picked them up, noticing how small they were. "Size nine!" he said out loud, looking at the tag. The last size he remembered his wife wearing was sixteen. He twirled them on his finger, then slingshot them directly into the trashcan, knowing LouAnn had probably worn them for somebody else.

When he opened the closet to find something to wear, he couldn't believe what he saw. His clothes had all been cleaned out. He started to break a sweat. He looked through her brand-new wardrobe. Some of it still had the price tags.

Gator found his clothes in a box in the spare bedroom. After he dressed himself in blue jeans and a tank top with "Let's Party" written on it, he opened his boys' bedroom door. Not one toy was out of place. That meant they hadn't been there all day either.

Gator looked in the icebox and found a cold beer between a loaf of bread and some leftover Honey Island Mudbug Jambalaya. "At least the woman ain't left me completely high and dry."

Honey Island Mudbug Jambalaya

1 tablespoon flour
2 tablespoons oil
1 cup chopped onions
1½ cups cold water
2½ cups peeled crawfish tails
1⅛ cups uncooked white rice
½ cup chopped parsley

½ cup chopped green onions
½ cup chopped celery
½ cup chopped bell pepper
2½ teaspoons salt
Black pepper to taste
Red pepper to taste

Make a roux with the flour and oil (see page 6). When the roux is dark brown, add the onions, stirring till they are almost cooked. Add the water and simmer for 30 minutes. Put in the crawfish tails and cook 10 to 15 minutes, until they turn pink.

Stir in the remaining ingredients. Cook on low heat, covered, for 30 minutes, or until rice is tender. Five minutes before serving, fluff with a fork.

Wood Duck Jambalaya

3 ducks, cleaned and cut up
½ pound ham, sliced or cubed
½ pound smoked sausage,
   sliced or cubed
6 tablespoons olive oil
2 tablespoons butter
3 onions, chopped
3 cloves garlic, minced
1 bell pepper, chopped

2 tablespoons chopped celery
4 tablespoons chopped parsley
8 cups canned chicken broth
3 bay leaves
Salt and hot pepper sauce
   to taste
Pinch of thyme
4 cups uncooked white rice

Lightly brown the ducks, ham, and sausage in the olive oil and butter. Add the onions, garlic, and bell pepper and sauté for a minute or two, stirring constantly. Add the remaining ingredients, except the rice, and simmer 45 minutes to 1 hour. Wash the rice and add it to the simmering mixture. Cook for about 15 minutes, tightly covered. The rice should be done, but not too soft. Add more chicken broth if needed.

West Pearl Jambalaya

1 cup chopped onions
1 tablespoon vegetable oil
1 pound ground beef
½ pound sausage, chopped
½ cup chopped celery
1 bell pepper, chopped
3 cloves garlic, mashed
1 teaspoon Worcestershire
  sauce

1 teaspoon cayenne pepper
1 (3-ounce) pack onion soup mix
1 cup water
3 large carrots, steamed
  and sliced
2 potatoes, cooked and cut up
1 (14-ounce) can cream of
  mushroom soup
2 cups cooked white rice

Sauté the onions in the oil until softened. Add the ground beef and sausage and cook until browned. Remove the onions and meat from the pan and set aside. Sauté the celery, bell pepper, and garlic in the same oil in the pan. Transfer the meat and onions back to the pan and add Worcestershire sauce and cayenne pepper. Stir.

Add the onion soup mix, water, remaining vegetables, and cream of mushroom soup. Cover and simmer for 30 minutes. Add the cooked rice and mix together without mashing the rice or vegetables.

The phone rang. Gator picked it up, "Yeah?" Silence. "Who the hell is this?" Gator asked.

"Uh, Gator, is that you?" LouAnn's mama asked, astonished, but not nearly as jolted as LouAnn would be.

"Who the hell you think it is?" he answered.

"I didn't know you was coming home," Nanny said, wondering how she would answer any questions he might ask about LouAnn.

"Where's my boys?"

"With me. LouAnn had to work all night, and I reckon she went shopping when she got off."

"You bring my boys home." Gator hung up, downed the beer, and then pitched the empty can into the paper sack sitting on the floor. He had done worked up an appetite so he took out the leftover jambalaya and sat down at the kitchen table.

Roxy carried out a heaping pan of hush puppies.

"Hey, Foxy," Darrel said on his way to the backyard.

Roxy froze in her tracks and grabbed Darrel's arm, "Darrel! Where's Gator?"

"I dropped him off at his house."

"Oh heck!" Roxy put the hush puppies on the picnic table and raced back inside.

Colleen was digging through the refrigerator looking for stuff to make the dipping sauce.

"Remind me to kill LouAnn when I see her," Roxy said.

"If Gator don't first," Colleen responded.

Spicy Dipping Sauce for Crawfish

5 tablespoons tartar sauce	2 squirts ketchup
3 tablespoons horseradish	½ teaspoon salt
3 green onions, chopped	Pepper to taste
1 teaspoon mustard	2 teaspoons hot sauce

Mix well. Keep adding stuff till it tastes right.

Gator looked at LouAnn's dusty old Cutlass sitting in the yard. "I hope she's having a good time in my truck," he thought.

Nanny's station wagon rolled into the driveway. The door opened and Ollie and Dusty climbed out, racing for their daddy's arms. Gator picked up his boys.

"Daddy, you're home!" they cried.

"Y'all been good?" Gator ask. He looked at Nanny, who stood there smiling, knowing her grandchildren missed their daddy like crazy.

Meanwhile, LouAnn drove the truck down Pontchartrain Drive listening to WNOE country music radio. She ripped the price tag off her brand-new blouse. She'd been to the mall and bought something pretty to wear that night and changed in the dressing room after she paid for it. When she stopped at a red light, she dug deep into her crochet purse, whipped out a can of hair spray, and teased her bleached blond hair as high as she could, gluing it in place. Then she found her cigarettes. Before she lit up, she remembered how Gator used to warn her about her hair exploding if it got too close to fire, so she kept the match at a distance. She did all this before the light turned green.

LouAnn was meeting Charles at his friend's condo in Eden Isles, which was one of the fanciest neighborhoods on the waterfront. They were going to have an early cocktail. LouAnn needed a cocktail just thinking about being introduced to perfect strangers by a man who was almost a perfect stranger himself. So she stopped at the Pic-a-Pack for a one of them mixed drinks in the bottle to loosen up. She wondered if she should bring a bottle of strawberry wine, which is about the nicest wine you can buy at the Pic-a-Pack. She decided against it. "They probably drink that sparklin' water." LouAnn talked out loud to herself in tense situations. Before she got back in her truck, she put a quarter in the pay phone and called her mama's house. There was no answer.

As LouAnn drove out to Eden Isles she starts contemplating how she couldn't get remarried till she gets divorced and how long that would take if Gator didn't agree on it. Then the thought of telling Gator she wanted a divorce made her a little sad. He had got a good side when he wanted to. But then she remembered how mad she was at him for being so darn stupid, robbing poor Mr. Bo James, who used to give her free bubble gum when she was little.

LouAnn parked in front of the fancy condo and double-checked the address she'd written on a napkin from the Chicken Poop. "This is it." LouAnn shoved the empty mixed drink bottle underneath her seat, slipped on her spiked heels, and got out. She pulled her tight jeans out of where they don't belong, took a deep breath, and strutted to the door. She knocked. The door was opened by a high-class woman flashing a hokey smile, the kind you see on TV commercials. "You must be LouAnn," the woman said, still showing off her perfect, white teeth.

"Yep, that's me."

"Come in. Charles is outside by the boat with Richard," her hostess, Ashly, said. She led her through the condo quickly, not giving LouAnn time to look at all the nice decorations. "Can I get you a glass of wine?" Ashly politely offers.

"Yes, thank you."

"Red or white?" Ashly asked, putting LouAnn on the spot—she'd never been offered a choice of color before at somebody's house, and she really didn't know the difference.

"Uh, red," LouAnn answered.

"You can join Charles while I pour it. We have appetizers on the table outside."

LouAnn saw Charles deep in conversation with Richard, standing on the yacht parked at the pier. She marveled at how a boat that big and fancy would get to the camp up the Pearl River. Charles waved to LouAnn when he noticed her standing on the deck. He was a handsome man, wearing Ralph Lauren and smoking a fine cigar. LouAnn waved back at him, wondering how she ended up with a man that looked like he came from a soap opera. Then she checks out the appetizer table. There was no coleslaw or macaroni salad, not even any potato chips among the funny-looking little mushrooms stuffed with who-knows-what and a plate of something else she had never seen before. It was just as well, because she was on a diet. She suddenly remembered Scooter's crawfish boil that her boys wanted to go to. LouAnn hadn't mentioned to Charles that she had two kids. Maybe tonight would be the night. Maybe she would convince Charles to go to the crawfish boil with her, test him out, see if he had got what it took to stand his ground with her family.

Charles introduced LouAnn to his friend Richard. LouAnn extended her hand as if she expected him to kiss it, but he just shook it instead. LouAnn was embarrassed for assuming all gentlemen were like the ones in the movies. Richard had the same accent as Charles—and it wasn't Southern. Charles told her once where he was from, but she couldn't pronounce it so she didn't remember it—somewhere in Maine.

"Charles tells me that he met you at a place called the Chicken Poop Lounge," Richard said to LouAnn.

"That's right."

Richard burst into laughter. Charles didn't expect Richard to embarrass LouAnn like that.

LouAnn suddenly felt out of place, not that she felt in place to start with. She was starting to get a hot flash when Ashly handed her the glass of red wine. LouAnn downed every last drop of it, scowling at the bitter taste. "They musta forgot the sugar in that batch," she said, wiping her mouth dry.

Back at Scooter's, the boys on stage were playing an old Waylon and Willie song. Some women started a line dance out on the lawn. The men sat around watching.

The water was at a full roaring boil so Scooter poured in the live mudbugs, which didn't stay live long.

Roxy was starting to loosen up, sipping on her Cypress Knee Daiquiri. She decided to let LouAnn handle her own problems, and boy did she have one!

58

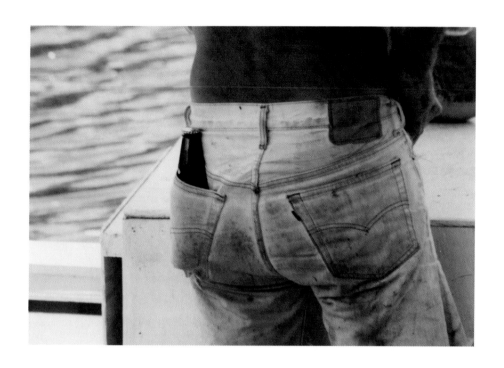

In Eden Isles, the conversation had drifted to small talk, boring LouAnn half to death. Ashly hadn't said one interesting thing since she'd gotten there. All she talked about was the humidity and some fund raiser she was organizing in the French Quarter. LouAnn thought about Scooter's crawfish boil—she hated missing out on the fun. "Charles, can we go?" LouAnn interrupted their conversation, and didn't give Charles a chance to decide if he wanted to go with her. "Thanks for your hospitality," she said to Ashly and Richard on her way out. Charles apologized behind LouAnn's back as he left.

Scooter's backyard shindig was hopping. He scooped out the first batch of fire-hot mudbugs and dumped them on top of the newspaper. Everyone dug in.

Suddenly the chatter ceased. Gator came walking up with his two boys. Scooter ran up and gave him a big bear hug. "Man, it's good to see you."

The other men took turns shaking his hand (if they weren't on hugging terms). The women kissed his cheek, complimenting him on his good looks, and the noise level returns to normal. Roxy walked out of her house and saw Gator standing there. She pulled herself together and gave him a hug. "Welcome home, stranger."

"You looking fine as ever, Foxy," Gator commented in front of Scooter, who appreciates his compliment. He knew about their affair ten years ago, but that was water over the bridge.

"Ain't you gonna give your sister a hug?" Colleen yelled, arms spread. Gator lifted her off the ground like he always did when he hadn't seen her in a while.

Gator glanced around the party crowd looking for you-know-who.

"Darrel, get Gator a cold beer," Scooter ordered.

"Y'all don't have no whiskey 'round here, do you?" Gator asked.

A hush fell over the crowd. Then Gator cracked a smile, "I was just kiddin'!"

Scooter slapped him on the back. "At least you ain't lost your since of humor."

"Wait till LouAnn gets here," Roxy muttered to Mona.

LouAnn's parked her shiny truck on the road. Charles looked a bit worried about the whole situation. "Now don't worry, this is my brother's house," LouAnn told him as she painted her lips pink.

Charles had no idea what he was about to walk into. "It can't be much different than the Chicken Poop Lounge."

LouAnn glanced at him, knowing better. "Do you run fast?" she asked, suddenly realizing she shouldn't have.

"Why?"

She giggled, although she was sort of serious. "Come on, you'll be fine."

The music was blasting on stage, Gator was shooting the breeze with his buddies, and Scooter was dumping the second batch of crawdads on the picnic table. Eyes began to move to the driveway.

Roxy saw LouAnn leading Charles through the gate. "Oh, Lord oh mighty. The world's 'bout to come to an end," Roxy mumbled to herself.

Scooter noticed, too. "LouAnn's done lost her mind," he said to Bubba.

Gator slowly turned to see what had everybody's attention.

LouAnn thought they were just surprised she was bringing a man to Scooter's house. She had no idea that Gator was there.

LouAnn didn't even see Gator because he was standing behind the line dancers.

"Why's everybody staring at us like that?" Charles asked LouAnn as they approached the crowd.

"They're just curious is all." She tried to comfort him.

Roxy met them halfway. "Gator's here," Roxy whispered to LouAnn.

"What?" LouAnn thought she heard wrong.

"Your husband's done got out the pen," Roxy whispered.

LouAnn almost fainted. Roxy held on to her arm. "I think you should turn your butt around and get on down the road with this man."

But it was too late. LouAnn's eyes met with Gator's, who had moved into her view.

"Gator! You're out of jail!" LouAnn said, as dazed as a newborn baby.

"Hey, darlin'. Who's your friend?" Gator asked, eyeing Charles.

"He's my lawyer."

"Your lawyer! What do you need a lawyer for?"

LouAnn thought quickly, "'Cause I might want a divorce."

Charles almost choked, he had no idea LouAnn was married, much less married to an ex-con.

"A divorce!" Gator burst into laughter. "You plannin' to put me on trial right here tonight?" Gator asked.

"I just might," LouAnn said boldly.

Gator extended his hand to Charles. "I'm LouAnn's husband. I s'pose she ain't told you 'bout me, by the confused look on your face, so I ain't holdin' no grudges against you. Why don't you go get yourself a drink and stick around a while. I might need a good attorney when I get through with her," Gator says to Charles with the biggest grin anyone had seen all night.

"Uh, LouAnn, maybe this isn't a good idea," Charles said, about to turn and run.

"Shore it is. Come on in and have some crawfish, too. Scooter's done boiled up a new batch," Gator said, practically yanking Charles into the backyard. He grabbed LouAnn's arm too, dragging her with them. He noticed her thin arms. "You're too durn skinny, woman."

"Let go of my arm, Gator!" LouAnn demanded, yanking away.

"I just got outta jail. Y'all can help me celebrate," Gator suggested, puzzling LouAnn even more than she already was. She thought Gator must be up to something, because he was not being himself.

Gator led them to the picnic table while all eyes were fixed on them. "Dig in, Charles," Gator said, practically forcing Charles to eat. Then he took LouAnn aside. "S'cuse us a minute, Charles. I'd like a private word with my old lady."

Charles didn't dare interfere, especially since he was outnumbered.

Scooter decided to make Charles feel at home, since after all, he was an innocent bystander. "You need a drink. Foxy, hun, fix this man one of your famous daiquiris. He's gonna need it."

Cypress Knee Daiquiri

Cypress knees are dead tree stumps that stick out of the water (or hide just below the surface) down in the river and bayous. You've got to be careful of them when you're swimming or boating. Make sure you're not standing around any cypress knees when you drink these daiquiris. We wouldn't want no nasty accidents!

In a blender, combine a scoop of vanilla ice cream, 2 shots of vodka, 2 or 3 shots of rum, ½ cup pineapple juice, ½ cup orange juice, a squeeze of lime, a dozen fresh strawberries, another shot of rum and vodka, and fill the rest of the blender with ice cubes. Mix till it tastes right.

Gator led LouAnn out of earshot from everyone who wished they could hear. Of course, as much gossiping as would get done afterwards, they'd all learn what happened.

"Woman, what the hell are you doin'?" Gator asked LouAnn.

"You left me with two kids to take care of and a bunch of bills. Every now and then I need somebody to give me some attention."

Gator looked over at Charles. "And you disgraced me by picking somebody like that?"

"He's a nice man, Gator. He don't rob stores and he don't get drunk," LouAnn told him.

"I guess he's the reason you stopped comin' to see me, ain't he?"

"No. I stopped comin' because seein' you there depressed me too much."

"Depressed you! What about me? I was the one stuck in that dungeon for six months."

"Well, it's your own durn fault," she said, matter-of-factly.

"I know, baby doll," Gator's voice softened.

LouAnn looked at him more closely, now really suspicious. It had been years since he called her baby doll. "You feel alright?" she asked.

"I missed you. I had a lot of time to think in there, and I realized that you're the most important thing in my life, you and the kids. And I promised myself I would never mix whiskey with wine again. And the only time I'm gonna handle a gun is when I go huntin'," Gator told her.

LouAnn couldn't believe it. She scratched her head, wondering if he learned some kind of psychology in jail. "You're acting awful funny."

"That's 'cause I love you so much, and if you leave me for that fancy business man over there, I'm just gonna shoot myself," Gator said with the most love LouAnn had ever heard from him, except when he asked her to marry him twelve years ago.

"Oh, Gator! I love you too!" LouAnn cried out, wrapping her arms around him.

Everyone looked over, not believing their eyes—especially Charles, who downed enough of the daiquiri to give himself an instant cold headache.

Scooter patted Charles on the back. "Welcome to the swamp. Wanna 'nother one?" Scooter asked, grinning ear to ear.

"I do believe I will," Charles answered gratefully as Roxy poured the effective mixture from the old milk jug.

LouAnn apologized to Charles for any inconvenience she might have caused him, and Gator forgave Charles for any actions he took with his wife before now. Then he told Charles to keep in touch, because you never know what can happen in the future and he might need a good lawyer one of these days.

Charles didn't know what to think about all that, so he sat in a lawn chair watching the band wind down and drinking another daiquiri.

Most of the crowd lived within walking distance, for those that were too drunk to drive home. And thank goodness, because here comes Leroy, strutting up in his perfectly pressed police uniform, twiddling a toothpick in his teeth.

"Look who it is," Mona said to Roxy as they cleaned up before they called it a night.

"Howdy!" Leroy said to the ladies.

"You're late, Leroy. You missed the fun," Roxy informed him.

"I had some earlier. I jist wanted to stop by and check on thangs," he said as he inspected the remaining crowd, seeing Gator and LouAnn slow dancing under the magnolia tree. "Ain't they cute?" Then he noticed Charles passed out in the lawn chair. "Who's he?"

"That's a New Orleans lawyer."

"He's drunk as a coot is what he is," Leroy detected.

"Don't worry, Leroy, we ain't lettin' him drive home," Roxy said.

Scooter walked up. "Leroy, how 'bout a drink to round off your night?"

"Nah, I got to get on back to town," Leroy says as Gator gave him the finger. Leroy smiled, knowing Gator was bound to mess up again sooner or later. "Well, I'll be seein' y'all."

The party crowd was clearing out. Colleen had to be carried to the truck by Earl. She had too much homemade wine. But even in her drunken state, she has never let go of her favorite Mardi Gras plastic cup.

LouAnn and Gator snuck home to ravish each other since they just lived down the road, and their kids were asleep in Scooter and Roxy's living room.

"Whatta 'bout him?" Roxy asked, motioning at Charles.

Scooter said, "I'll take him home in the mornin'."

"I hope the mosquitoes don't eat him alive out here," Roxy worried.

"He's got too much booze in his blood. They won't touch him," Scooter said, an authority on such information. He wrapped his arms around Roxy, "Well, Foxy, hun. Whatta you say we go get snug as a bug in the rug?"

CHAPTER FOUR

Side Dishes and Sweet Stuff

Joan and Smokey's Sandbar Wedding

This event went down in Louisiana history. Joan and Smokey tied the knot under a cypress tree on the Pearl River Sandbar (the one Denty Crawford cleared off for partying) with an audience of a hundred or so that had to get there by boat. That party was quite different—but only because the justice of the peace showed up. The newspaper photographer even came and took pictures that ran on a full page.

The bride was brought upriver by boat, in her white sundress and straw hat, and the groom and his best man waited on the sandbar dressed in black tank tops and black shorts with bowtie, baseball caps, and flip-flops (the groom got married barefooted). The audience was dressed in shorts and bathing suits. When the bride was helped off the boat, the crowd gathered around ankle deep in sand to witness the event. After they were married and the bride kissed the groom, everybody ate, swam, and cut up in the shade.

Nana's Gumbo

Nana (Yvonne Ford) has always been my favorite cook. She was raised in Napoleonville, Louisiana, where she learned to cook first-hand from her Cajun mother. I used to listen to them ramble on in Cajun French while they made gumbo. I didn't understand a word they said, but I sure did like what they were brewing in that big black iron pot. Here is Nana's gumbo recipe.

¼ cup vegetable oil
1 cup flour
1½ cups chopped white onion
1 cup chopped bell pepper
1 cup chopped celery
6 cloves garlic, chopped
2 pounds fresh or frozen okra
2 quarts cold water
2 bay leaves
2½ teaspoons cayenne pepper

Salt and pepper to taste
4 drops Tabasco sauce
2 pounds shrimp, peeled, cleaned, and deveined
1 pound canned crab meat
2 pints raw oysters
¼ cup chopped parsley
1 cup chopped green onions
2 cups white rice
Filé, for garnish

First, make a roux with the oil and flour (see page 6). When the roux is dark brown, add the white onion, bell pepper, celery, garlic, and okra and cook, stirring occasionally, until the okra is softened. Then add the 2 quarts water, bay leaves, salt and pepper, and Tabasco sauce, bring to a boil, and let simmer for 40 minutes.

Add the shrimp, crab meat, and oysters to the mixture, bring to a boil, and cook for 10 minutes more. Remove the mixture from the heat and add the parsley and green onions. Serve with the rice and sprinkle with filé.

Nana's Smothered Okra

¼ cup vegetable oil
10 pounds okra, washed
   and sliced ½ inch thick
2 large bell peppers, chopped
2 large onions, chopped

2 (14-ounce) cans stewed
   tomatoes, or 4 fresh
   tomatoes, peeled
Salt and pepper to taste

Pour the oil into a big, heavy pan. Make sure you use enough to cover the bottom. Add the okra, bell peppers, and onions and mix. Cover tightly and bake at 300° for 1 hour. Add the tomatoes and stir until blended. Re-cover and continue baking for at least 2 more hours. Stir occasionally to prevent sticking. When cooked, add salt and pepper and serve.

Uncle Perry's Fried Dill Pickles

1 cup whole milk	1 cup flour
1 egg	Salt and pepper to taste
1 cup cornmeal	1 jar sliced dill pickles

Mix the milk and egg to make the wet batter. For the dry batter, combine the cornmeal, flour, and salt and pepper. Dip the sliced dill pickles into the wet batter first and then the dry batter. Deep-fry them till they rise to the top of the oil and the batter turns golden brown.

Uncle Perry's Fried Sardines

1 cup whole milk	1 cup flour
1 egg	Salt and pepper to taste
1 cup cornmeal	1 can whole sardines

Mix the milk and egg to make the wet batter. Combine the cornmeal and flour to make the dry batter. Add salt and pepper to the dry batter. Gently remove the sardines from the can and dip them into the wet batter. Then gently dip them into the dry batter. Deep-fry the sardines till they float to the top of the oil and the batter turns golden brown.

Landmarks in Honey Island Swamp

There are a couple of landmarks in the swamp that you might want to check out if you have the chance. The first spot is a cypress tree at Davis Landing with a pair of false teeth nailed to it to commemorate a little mishap in the summer of '97. The real teeth that were there before belonged to Dave. On one particular afternoon, Dave crashed into that cypress tree.

Dave was at the camp having a little drink with the guys, when word came that a girl in a bikini was waiting at the boat landing for a ride to the camp. The guys volunteered Dave to go get her. A few

others were volunteered as well, and the race was on. The men jumped into their boats before the messenger finished the message. The spectators waited at the camp to see who this mystery girl in the bikini was. Fifteen minutes passed and the girl never showed—neither did Dave nor the other contenders. But it wasn't because somebody got to her first; it was because Dave didn't see the cypress tree when he cut around the bend at thirty or so miles an hour. His mouth hit the tree and his teeth stayed there. He had to go to the hospital for X-rays and stitches. After all that commotion, the girl in the bikini finally got a ride to the camp with somebody else, and everybody found out that the message was suppose to be delivered to Mr. Dan in the first place, because she had come to see him. Mr. Dan could have saved Dave a lot of pain and a few teeth had he known, but as he said, "That's what some folks get for jumpin' the gun."

Uncle Perry's Swamp Basting Sauce

1 large onion, chopped
½ bulb garlic, chopped
1 cup olive oil
1 (3-ounce) bag crab boil
1 (8-ounce) bottle Louisiana
    Hot Sauce

2 cups coffee, dripped and black
1 cup apple cider vinegar
1 cup Worcestershire sauce
1 lemon, halved

Sauté the onion and garlic in the olive oil. Add everything else but the lemons. Squeeze the 2 lemon halves into the sauce, then drop the peels in. Cook over medium heat for 30 minutes, stirring constantly. Take the crab boil bag out when you're done. Use the sauce to baste chicken, roast, or whatever!

Uncle Perry's Come-Back Dipping Sauce

1 cup mayonnaise
6 cloves garlic, finely minced

Salt and pepper to taste
1 squirt Louisiana Hot Sauce

Mix the ingredients a day ahead of time so the flavor is strong. Use it as a dipping sauce for fish, crawfish, shrimp, frog legs, or whatever you caught that day.

Uncle Perry's Dill Tartar Sauce

½ cup mayonnaise
¼ cup cream cheese
1 tablespoon lemon juice
3 tablespoons dill pickle juice
½ onion, finely chopped

2 cloves garlic, finely chopped
20 dill slices, finely chopped
¼ teaspoon cayenne pepper
1 teaspoon salt

Combine ingredients and blend till creamy.

Wild Wanda's Red Beans and Rice

1 pound red beans, washed	⅓ bell pepper, chopped
¾ pound wild boar sausage, chopped	Salt and pepper to taste
1 onion, minced	2 cups cooked white rice

Soak beans overnight in water. In the same water they soaked in, bring them to a boil, then lower the heat and let them simmer for 1½ hours. Add the sausage, onion, bell pepper, and salt and pepper and simmer another 1½ hours, until the beans and pork are tender. Serve over rice.

The Legendary Honey Island Swamp Monster

Way back before my day, my grandfather, Harlan E. Ford, was on foot deep in the Honey Island Swamp with his friend Billy. They were heading to a campsite they saw from the twin-engine plane Harlan had flown over the swamp. With their backpacks over their shoulders and guns in their cases, Harlan and Billy saw several wild boars that had their throats torn out for no apparent reason. Suspicious about what did this to the hogs, Harlan and Billy observed the area. But nothing stirred, so they kept on walking. Then they came upon something at the watering hole. "What is that, Harlan?" Billy asked.

The strange creature swung around and faced them, then stood up on two feet. Harlan and Billy went for their guns, but before they could get to them the eerie creature ran off. Harlan and Billy went after it, but there was no sign of the thing they saw. Harlan thought the creature may have dived into a slough. A few days later Harlan and Billy went back to the same watering hole with plaster of paris and made molds of the creature's footprints. Harlan contacted the LSU Zoology Department, who could not identify the tracks. LSU

called the Smithsonian Institute in Washington, DC, and two anthropologists flew to New Orleans to take a look at the odd-looking tracks. But they could not say what made them. The creature's tracks were the size of a man's foot and had four webbed toes.

Harlan described the creature as having short dingy hair on its body and long mossy hair on its head. He said its large wide-set eyes were amber—eyes he'd never forget.

Another old trapper known as Old Man Williams spent all his life in the Honey Island Swamp, and he claimed to have seen the same creature several times. He could have killed it but didn't because the creature didn't seem to want to harm him. Needless to say, a few years later Old Man Williams came up missing in Honey Island and was never heard from again.

The legend of the swamp monster lives on in Louisiana. There are those that think it's a hoax, but there are also those who believe—because they have seen it too.

Barbara's Swamped Pork'n'Beans

1 pound bacon
1 large onion, chopped
1 (1-gallon) can pork
   and beans

½ cup brown sugar
1 (14-ounce) can fruit
   cocktail
½ cup barbecue sauce

Fry the bacon and onions together in a skillet. Put the pork'n'beans into a baking pan. Add the brown sugar, fruit cocktail, and barbecue sauce, and mix well. Add the bacon and onions, and a little bacon grease, and mix. Bake at 400° for 45 minutes, or till the fruit cocktail is burnt on top.

Swamp Dressing Casserole

1 (2-pound) package wide
   egg noodles
1 white onion, chopped
3 cloves garlic, chopped
1 cup sliced mushrooms
1 stick butter
1 (14-ounce) can mackerel or
   2 (6-ounce) cans tuna

8 ounces mild cheddar cheese,
   grated
1 tablespoon soy sauce
Salt to taste
2 or 3 tablespoons hot sauce
1 (14-ounce) can chili (no beans)
1 cup corn flakes, crushed

Boil the egg noodles. Sauté the onion, garlic, and mushrooms in the butter. Mix the egg noodles with the onion, garlic, and mushrooms. Add the fish, cheese (reserving some for the top), soy sauce, salt, and hot sauce. Mix well. Pour the mixture into a baking pan. Pour the chili on top. Add the remaining grated cheese and then the corn flakes. Bake for 40 minutes at 350°.

Blue Crab Delight

1½ sticks butter
1 bulb garlic, chopped
1 cup Wishbone Italian
    dressing

1 (12-ounce) can beer
2 tablespoons hot sauce
2 tablespoons chopped parsley
1 cup cooked crab meat

Melt the butter in a large saucepan. Add the garlic and sauté for a few minutes. Add the Wishbone dressing, beer, and hot sauce. Mix in the crab meat. Simmer for 30 minutes. Add parsley and serve with chips or crackers.

Joan's Cajun Chicken Wings

Deep-fry a dozen chicken wings, using no seasoning, until cooked through. While the wings are frying, heat 1 cup Louisiana Hot Sauce in a saucepan and add a little margarine. The more margarine you add, the less spicy the wings will be. Bring the sauce to a boil and cook for 5 minutes. When it cools, use it as a dipping sauce for the wings.

Muddy Water Rice and Chicken Parts

2 onions, chopped
2 stalks celery, chopped
4 green onions, chopped
3 tablespoons vegetable oil
¼ pound chicken gizzards,
    chopped or ground
¼ pound chicken livers,
    chopped or ground

1 pound ground beef
2 tablespoons chopped parsley
½ bouillon cube, dissolved
    in ½ cup hot water
Salt and pepper to taste
1 tablespoon Worcestershire
    sauce
3 cups cooked white rice

Sauté the onions, celery, and green onions in the oil until soft, at least 10 minutes. Add the gizzards, livers, ground meat, and parsley.

After browning the meat thoroughly, add the beef bouillon liquid, salt and pepper, and Worcestershire sauce. Cover and simmer over low heat for 30 minutes. Remove from the heat, add the rice, and mix well.

Cole's Wild Pheasant Soup

2 pheasants, cleaned and cut up
Salt and pepper to taste
1 cup white flour

¼ cup vegetable oil
6 large onions, chopped
2 cups cooked white rice

Season the pheasants with salt and pepper. Then coat them in flour like you're going to fry chicken. Put about ½ inch of cooking oil in a 16-inch iron frying pan. Brown the pheasant, about 10 minutes per side. Sauté the onions in the same pan, then return the pheasant to the pan. Pour in enough water to cover the pheasants. Simmer for 2 to 3 hours, till the water simmers down to ½ inch. Serve over rice.

Uncle Chuck's Barbecued Chittlins

2 feet chittlins, cleaned
   and cut into 3-inch pieces
2 teaspoons crab boil

Tony Chachere's Creole
   Seasoning to taste
Barbecue sauce

Boil the chittlins with the crab boil outside somewhere so the chittlins don't stink up the house. When they're tender, take them out of the pot and put them on a mesh screen over the barbecue pit. Sprinkle them with Tony Chachere's Creole Seasoning and then paint on barbecue sauce. Grill for about 30 minutes.

The Elks Lodge Double Wedding

A couple years ago, my little sister called me up. "Guess what?"

"What?" I asked.

"I'm gettin' married. And guess what else?" Danette said, excited.

"What?" I asked.

"So is Mark!" she said. Mark's our brother.

"At the same time?" I asked.

"Yep. Mom suggested we kill two birds with one stone, and she wanted to know if you had somebody you might wanna marry too, and get it all over with at once."

I did, but it would have been short notice. So I passed on the offer and she asked me to be her maid of honor instead.

I flew down to Louisiana to find all the women busy figuring out what they were gonna cook, even though we had hired a caterer. But we couldn't expect her to cook for as many River People as were going to show up. The invitations went out mostly by word of mouth, telling people to bring their friends if they wanted to. And they did. There's not much else to do down there besides go to the river or line dancing and look at the same old people, doing the same old thing. At a wedding, the River People get to look at the same old people dressed up in their Sunday best. They might even see a couple of new faces from out of town, and get free booze to boot.

The ceremony was held at the Elks Lodge Bingo Club. There was a gigantic stuffed elk head hanging on the wall above the preacher at rehearsal. I suggested they leave it up for character, but the brides wanted it covered with a white sheet and flowers.

The Elk Lodge owner supplied over two hundred aluminum folding chairs, and Daddy bought about five hundred dollars' worth of liquor, because he knew the River People could pour it down.

There were so many people, some had to stand up. The wedding was about to start, but the grooms and their best men were missing. I was sent out to find them, and there they were standing by their pickup trucks talking about squirrel hunting.

The wedding went pretty smoothly, except that the preacher went on and on—he liked to hear himself talk. He didn't really preach at a church anymore, so he was enjoying the audience. Finally the preacher said the brides could kiss the grooms, and then the festivity began. The band started up, the drinks were handed out, and the food was cleaned out in no time at all.

After we ate everything there was, we danced till the sheet came off the elk and the Elks Lodge owner kicked us out.

Barbara's Swamp Bread Pudding

3 loaves bread (French or sliced) ½ cup raisins
8 eggs 2 tablespoons cinnamon
½ cup vanilla Barbara's Damn Good Rum
½ pound sugar   Sauce (below)
1½ cups whole milk

Mix all the ingredients except the sauce till soupy. Pour into a greased baking pan and bake at 400° for 1 hour. When it's done, pour Barbara's Damn Good Rum Sauce over it and serve.

Barbara's Damn Good Rum Sauce

1 pound butter, melted 3 cups sugar
1 tablespoon vanilla 1 cup rum

Combine the butter, vanilla, sugar, and rum. Simmer till it gets thick. Pour over bread pudding.

Nana's Chocolate Sheet Cake

CAKE

2 sticks oleo

1 cup water

4 tablespoons cocoa

2 cups flour

2 cups sugar

1 tablespoon baking powder

½ teaspoon salt

2 eggs

1 teaspoon vanilla

1 teaspoon baking soda

½ cup buttermilk

ICING

1 stick oleo

4 tablespoons milk

4 tablespoons cocoa

3¾ confectioner's sugar

1 teaspoon vanilla

1 cup chopped nuts (optional)

In a saucepan, bring to a boil the oleo, water, and cocoa. Sift together the flour, sugar, baking powder, and salt into a mixing bowl. Pour the liquid mixture over the dry ingredients and mix well. In a separate bowl, beat together the eggs and vanilla. Add the baking soda to the buttermilk, stir, and combine with the egg mixture. Then add the egg mixture to the other ingredients and mix well.

Pour the batter into two greased 9½-x-11-inch pans, and bake 20 minutes at 400°.

When cake has been baking 10 minutes, begin preparing the icing. Bring to a boil the oleo, milk, and cocoa. Place the confectioner's sugar in a bowl, pour the liquid mixture over it, add the vanilla and nuts, and mix well.

Ice the cake in the pan while still hot. It may be necessary to add a little hot water to the icing to make it spread easily. Allow the iced cake to cool. Cut and serve directly from the pan.

Mom's Louisiana Mayhaw Jelly

Most people aren't lucky enough to have a mayhaw tree in their backyard. If you're one of those unfortunate souls, you'll have to go into the swamp. You can usually find a tree off of a river or creek bed. The saying is, "If they bloom over the water, they'll fall in the water" (the water is usually high when they're in bloom). If you find a mayhaw tree over the water, knock the berries into the water and scoop them out. When you get home, remove the stems and blossom end. You don't necessarily have to remove all the stems. Just make sure the berries are clean and that unhealthy berries are thrown out.

First, sterilize the jars, lids, and caps in hot boiling water.

Then combine one-half pot of mayhaw berries and one-half pot of water. Bring this to a boil and continue to boil till they're soft enough to mash. Take the pot off the fire. Dip the berries into cheesecloth or an old pillow case. Squeeze the berries into the pot till you get every drop of juice out of them. That puts all the flavor back in the pot.

Now you're ready to make the jelly. Have your sterilized jars and lids ready. Mix 3½ cups of juice to 5 cups of water. Add 1 box of gelatin. Bring the mixture to a rolling boil, cook for 1 minute, and remove from the heat.

After the mixture has set for 3 to 5 minutes, skim the foam from the top. (Some people add ½ teaspoon of butter when adding the gelatin to keep the mixture from foaming. This is optional.) Then fill the jars ⅛ inch from the top. Use a paper towel to wipe the rims of the jars to remove any liquid that might have gotten on them. Cover the jars quickly with lids and screw the caps on tight. Turn jars upside down for 5 minutes. Then turn them back upright. After the jars have cooled, check the seals by pressing the middle of the lid with your finger. If the lid springs up, it is not sealed. After jars are sealed, let them sit at room temperature for 24 hours. Then the jelly is done.

Intoxicated Yams

6 yams, peeled and cubed
½ cup butter or oleo
1 cup apple cider
⅓ cup dark rum
¼ cup brown sugar, packed

¼ teaspoon salt
¼ teaspoon allspice
¼ teaspoon mace
1 teaspoon ground ginger
⅓ cup raisins

Place the yams in a 2-quart buttered casserole dish. Put the butter, apple cider, rum, brown sugar, salt, allspice, mace, and ginger in a saucepan over medium heat. Stir until the butter has melted and the sugar has dissolved into a syrup. Pour about half of this syrup over the yams. Sprinkle the raisins over the top and pour the remaining syrup over the raisins and yams.

Cover tightly and bake for 1 hour at 325°. Increase the heat to 425°, uncover the casserole, and bake about 30 minutes more, or till the juices are bubbling.

Wanda's Whiskey Cake

3 eggs
1 pound white sugar
½ pound butter
½ pound brown sugar

3 cups flour
½ teaspoon mace
¼ pint whiskey
½ cup broken pecans

Mix the eggs and white sugar, beating well. Cream the butter with the brown sugar using an electric mixer. Combine the egg mixture with the butter mixture.

Sift in the flour and mace, then add the whiskey and pecans. Bake in a tube pan at 300° for 1½ hours. (Note: This cake should have a moist crumbly texture. Wrap it in foil and store it in a cool place. Do not freeze it. It will last 2 or 3 weeks.)

Index

Ordering and Shipping Mudbugs and Seafood

To have alligator, blue crab, crabmeat, crawfish, froglegs, oysters, shrimp, soft-shell crab, turtle, cajun sausage, gumbo, and more delivered fresh to your door overnight anywhere in the country, contact New Orleans Over Night, Inc. (800) NU-AWLINS; www.nuawlins.com.